Oven-Free Classics

No-bake delights everyone will love

double-dipped strawberries

PREP: 10 min. | TOTAL: 10 min. | MAKES: 10 servings, 1 dipped strawberry each.

▶ what you need!

10 fresh strawberries (about 1 pt.), washed, well dried

4 squares BAKER'S Semi-Sweet Chocolate, melted

8 OREO Cookies, coarsely crushed (about 1 cup crumbs)

▶ make it!

1. **DIP** strawberries in melted chocolate; roll in crumbs.

2. **PLACE** on waxed paper-covered baking sheet; let stand until chocolate is firm.

SUBSTITUTE:
Prepare using BAKER'S Premium White Chocolate.

EASY MICROWAVE MELTING OF BAKER'S CHOCOLATE SQUARES:
Microwave 1 unwrapped square of BAKER'S Chocolate in microwaveable bowl on HIGH 1 min., stirring after 30 sec. or until chocolate is almost melted. (The square will retain its shape.) Stir 1 min. or until chocolate is completely melted. Add 10 sec. for each additional square of chocolate, stirring every 30 sec.

angel lush with pineapple

PREP: 15 min. | TOTAL: 1 hour 15 min. | MAKES: 10 servings.

▶ what you need!

1 can (20 oz.) DOLE Crushed Pineapple in Juice, undrained

1 pkg. (3.4 oz.) JELL-O Vanilla Flavor Instant Pudding

1 cup thawed COOL WHIP Whipped Topping

1 pkg. (10 oz.) round angel food cake, cut into 3 layers

1 cup fresh mixed berries

▶ make it!

1. **MIX** pineapple and dry pudding mix. Gently stir in COOL WHIP.

2. **STACK** cake layers on plate, spreading pudding mixture between layers and on top of cake.

3. **REFRIGERATE** 1 hour. Top with berries.

   DOLE is a registered trademark of Dole Food Company, Inc.

   VARIATION:
   Prepare using 1 pkg. (1 oz.) JELL-O Vanilla Flavor Fat Free Sugar Free Instant Pudding and COOL WHIP LITE Whipped Topping.

   HOW TO CUT CAKE:
   Use toothpicks to mark cake into 3 layers. Use a serrated knife to cut cake, in sawing motion, into layers.

   LEMON-BERRY LUSH WITH PINEAPPLE:
   Prepare using JELL-O Lemon Flavor Instant Pudding.

OREO ice cream shop pie

PREP: 15 min. | TOTAL: 4 hours 15 min. | MAKES: 10 servings.

▶ what you need!

½ cup hot fudge ice cream topping, divided

1 OREO Pie Crust (6 oz.)

1 tub (8 oz.) COOL WHIP Whipped Topping, thawed, divided

2 pkg. (4.2 oz. each) JELL-O OREO Flavor Instant Pudding

1¼ cups cold milk

▶ make it!

1. **RESERVE** 2 Tbsp. fudge topping; spread remaining topping onto bottom of crust. Cover with half the COOL WHIP. Freeze 10 min.

2. **BEAT** pudding mixes and milk in large bowl with whisk 2 min. (Mixture will be thick.) Stir in remaining COOL WHIP; spoon over COOL WHIP layer in crust.

3. **FREEZE** 4 hours or until firm. Remove pie from freezer 15 min. before serving. Let stand at room temperature to soften slightly. Drizzle with reserved fudge topping.

MAKE IT EASY:
If fudge topping is cold, remove cap and microwave topping on HIGH 30 sec. or until easy to spread.

HOW TO DRIZZLE CHOCOLATE:
Spoon chocolate topping into resealable plastic bag. Use scissors to cut off tiny piece from one bottom corner of bag. Twist top of bag and gently squeeze bag to drizzle chocolate over pie.

tall caramel-banana 'n pecan pie

PREP: 15 min. | TOTAL: 2 hours 15 min. | MAKES: 8 servings.

▶ what you need!

2 pkg. (8 oz. each) PHILADELPHIA Cream Cheese, softened

½ cup packed brown sugar

1 tsp. vanilla

1 tub (8 oz.) COOL WHIP Whipped Topping, thawed, divided

½ cup caramel ice cream topping, divided

1 HONEY MAID Graham Pie Crust (6 oz.)

½ cup PLANTERS Pecan Pieces, divided

2 bananas, sliced

▶ make it!

1. **BEAT** cream cheese, sugar and vanilla in large bowl with mixer until blended. Stir in 2 cups whipped topping with whisk; set aside.

2. **SPREAD** ¼ cup caramel topping onto bottom of crust; top with layers of ¼ cup pecans, bananas and cream cheese mixture. Cover with remaining whipped topping and pecans.

3. **REFRIGERATE** 2 hours. Drizzle with remaining caramel topping just before serving.

SIZE-WISE:
Sweets can be part of a balanced diet but remember to keep tabs on portions.

SPECIAL EXTRA:
Toast the pecans before using as directed. Garnish with additional PLANTERS Pecan Pieces and additional banana slices just before serving.

frosty orange dream squares

PREP: 20 min. | TOTAL: 3 hours 20 min. | MAKES: 24 servings, 1 square each.

▶ what you need!

40 NILLA Wafers, finely crushed (about 1½ cups)

¼ cup (½ stick) butter, melted

2 cups cold milk

2 pkg. (4-serving size each) JELL-O Vanilla Flavor Instant Pudding (see note below)

1 tub (8 oz.) COOL WHIP Whipped Topping, thawed, divided

2 cups orange sherbet, softened

▶ make it!

1. **LINE** 13×9-inch pan with foil, with ends of foil extending over sides of pan. Mix wafer crumbs and butter. Press onto bottom of prepared pan; set aside.

2. **ADD** milk to dry pudding mixes in medium bowl. Beat with wire whisk 2 min. or until well blended. Gently stir in half of the whipped topping. Spoon evenly over crust. Refrigerate 10 min. Add remaining whipped topping to sherbet; stir with wire whisk until well blended. Spoon over pudding layer; cover.

3. **FREEZE** at least 3 hours. Use foil handles to remove dessert from pan before cutting into squares to serve. Garnish as desired. Store leftovers in freezer.

NOTE FROM THE KRAFT KITCHENS:
For best texture, do not prepare recipe with JELL-O Fat Free Sugar Free Instant Pudding.

FROSTY ORANGE DREAM PIE:
Prepare as directed, substituting 1 HONEY MAID Graham Pie Crust (6 oz.) for the homemade crust and cutting all remaining ingredients in half.

SUBSTITUTE:
Prepare as directed, using lemon or lime sherbet and/or COOL WHIP LITE Whipped Topping.

chocolate frozen OREO bash

PREP: 15 min. | TOTAL: 3 hours 15 min. | MAKES: 16 servings.

▶ what you need!

16 OREO Cookies

2 squares BAKER'S Semi-Sweet Chocolate

1 pkg. (8 oz.) PHILADELPHIA Cream Cheese, softened

⅓ cup sugar

1 tub (6 oz.) COOL WHIP Chocolate Whipped Topping, thawed

¼ cup milk

▶ make it!

1. **ARRANGE** cookies in single layer on bottom of 8- or 9-inch square pan. Melt chocolate squares as directed on package; set aside.

2. **BEAT** cream cheese and sugar in large bowl with electric mixer on medium speed until well blended. Add chocolate; beat until well blended. Gently stir in whipped topping. Blend in milk. Pour over cookie layer in pan.

3. **FREEZE** several hours or until firm. Remove from freezer about 15 min. before serving; let stand in refrigerator until dessert can easily be cut. Store leftover dessert in freezer.

   SUBSTITUTE:
   Prepare as directed, using regular COOL WHIP Whipped Topping.

   JAZZ IT UP:
   Garnish with fresh raspberries, if desired.

"no-pan" ice cream sandwich dessert

PREP: 15 min. | TOTAL: 4 hours 15 min. | MAKES: 12 servings, 1 slice each.

▶ what you need!

½ cup fresh raspberries

½ cup sliced fresh strawberries

1 tub (8 oz.) COOL WHIP Whipped Topping, thawed, divided

12 rectangular vanilla ice cream sandwiches

▶ make it!

1. **PLACE** ½ cup each raspberries and strawberries in medium bowl. Mash lightly with fork. Gently stir in 1½ cups of the whipped topping.

2. **ARRANGE** 4 of the ice cream sandwiches, side-by-side, on 24-inch-long piece of foil; spread with half of the whipped topping mixture. Repeat layers. Top with remaining 4 ice cream sandwiches. Frost top and sides with remaining whipped topping. Bring up foil sides. Double fold top and ends to loosely seal packet.

3. **FREEZE** at least 4 hours before slicing to serve. Store leftovers in freezer.

JAZZ IT UP:
Prepare as directed, using Neapolitan ice cream sandwiches.

sweet peanut brittle

PREP: 5 min. | TOTAL: 50 min. | MAKES: About 1½ lb. or 16 servings.

▶ what you need!

1 cup sugar

½ cup light corn syrup

1 Tbsp. butter

2 cups PLANTERS COCKTAIL Peanuts

1 tsp. baking soda

1 tsp. vanilla

4 squares BAKER'S Semi-Sweet Chocolate

¼ cup creamy peanut butter

▶ make it!

1. **SPRAY** large baking sheet with cooking spray. Microwave sugar and corn syrup in large glass microwaveable bowl on HIGH 5 min. Stir in butter and peanuts. Microwave 3 to 4 min. or until pale golden brown. Stir in baking soda and vanilla. (Mixture will foam.) Spread onto prepared baking sheet. Cool completely. Break into pieces.

2. **MICROWAVE** chocolate in 1-cup glass measuring cup on HIGH 1 to 2 min. or until chocolate is melted when stirred. Add peanut butter; stir until melted. Dip half of each candy piece in chocolate mixture; scrape bottom against edge of cup to remove excess chocolate. Place on sheet of foil or waxed paper. Refrigerate 20 min. or until chocolate is firm.

SIZE-WISE:
Trying to pace your eating at a party? Preview your choices and be selective instead of taking some of everything.

CAUTION:
Use heavy oven mitts or potholders when removing bowl from microwave as candy mixture will be extremely hot. If available, use a 2-qt. glass measuring cup with handle as a large microwaveable bowl.

HOT/SWEET PEANUT BRITTLE:
Stir 1 tsp. hot pepper sauce into candy along with the vanilla.

NILLA-chocolate tiramisu cups

PREP: 30 min. | TOTAL: 4 hours 30 min. (incl. refrigerating) | MAKES: 12 servings.

▶ what you need!

- 4 squares BAKER'S Semi-Sweet Chocolate
- 1 Tbsp. butter or margarine
- 24 NILLA Wafers, divided
- 1 Tbsp. MAXWELL HOUSE Instant Coffee
- 2 Tbsp. hot water
- 1 pkg. (8 oz.) PHILADELPHIA Cream Cheese, softened
- ¼ cup sugar
- 1 tub (8 oz.) COOL WHIP Whipped Topping, thawed
- 6 fresh strawberries, halved

▶ make it!

1. **MICROWAVE** chocolate and butter in microwaveable bowl on HIGH 1½ min., stirring after 1 min. Stir until chocolate is completely melted. Spoon into 12 foil cup-lined muffin cups; brush chocolate onto bottom and halfway up side of each cup. Place 1 wafer in each cup. Refrigerate until ready to use.

2. **DISSOLVE** coffee in hot water. Place cream cheese and sugar in medium bowl. Gradually add coffee mixture, beating with whisk after each addition. Stir in whipped topping. Spoon ½ the cream cheese mixture into cups; top with remaining wafers and cream cheese mixture.

3. **REFRIGERATE** 4 hours or until set. Top with strawberries.

SPECIAL EXTRA:
Top each cup with an additional NILLA Wafer just before serving.

MAKE AHEAD:
Chocolate cups can be prepared ahead and stored, unfilled, in refrigerator up to 2 days.

OREO cookie cream pie

PREP: 30 min. | TOTAL: 4 hours 30 min. (incl. refrigerating) | MAKES: 10 servings.

▶ what you need!

24 OREO Chocolate Sandwich Cookies, divided

2 Tbsp. butter or margarine, melted

2 cups cold milk

2 pkg. (3.4 oz. each) JELL-O White Chocolate Flavor Instant Pudding & Pie Filling

2 cups thawed COOL WHIP Whipped Topping

½ cup fresh raspberries

½ square BAKER'S Semi-Sweet Chocolate, shaved into curls

▶ make it!

1. **CRUSH** 16 cookies. Mix with butter; press onto bottom and up side of 9-inch pie plate. Chop 8 remaining cookies; set aside.

2. **BEAT** milk and pudding mixes with whisk 2 min. Stir in whipped topping and chopped cookies. Spoon into crust. Refrigerate 4 hours.

3. **TOP** with raspberries and chocolate curls just before serving.

HOW TO MAKE CHOCOLATE CURLS:
Warm a square of BAKER'S Chocolate by microwaving it, unwrapped, on HIGH for a few seconds or just until you can smudge the chocolate with your thumb. Hold the square steadily and draw a peeler slowly over flat bottom of square, allowing a thin layer of chocolate to curl as it is peeled off the bottom of the square to make long, delicate curls. Use the same technique along the narrow side of the square to make short curls.

NILLA peppermint cremes

PREP: 30 min. | TOTAL: 3 hours 30 min. (incl. refrigerating) | MAKES: 10 servings.

▶ what you need!

4 squares BAKER'S Premium White Chocolate

2 Tbsp. whipping cream

1½ tsp. butter or margarine

6 drops peppermint extract

40 NILLA Wafers

4 starlight mints, crushed

▶ make it!

1. **MICROWAVE** chocolate, cream and butter in microwaveable bowl on HIGH 1 to 1½ min. or until butter is melted, stirring after 1 min. Stir until chocolate is completely melted. Blend in extract.

2. **REFRIGERATE** 3 hours or until firm.

3. **SHAPE** 1 tsp. of the chocolate mixture into ½-inch ball; place between 2 wafers to form sandwich. Press together gently. Roll edge in crushed candies; place on waxed paper-covered baking sheet. Repeat to make 20 cookie sandwiches.

HOW TO DOUBLE RECIPE:
This recipe can be easily doubled to make enough for a party. Just prepare as directed, doubling the chocolate, cream, butter, wafers and mints, and using ⅛ tsp. extract.

HOW TO STORE PEPPERMINT CREMES:
Store in tightly covered container in refrigerator up to 2 days.

CHIPS AHOY!
warm s'mores

PREP: 5 min. | TOTAL: 6 min. | MAKES: 8 servings.

▶ what you need!

16 CHIPS AHOY! Cookies, divided

2 squares BAKER'S Semi-Sweet Chocolate, chopped

2 tsp. BAKER'S ANGEL FLAKE Coconut

16 JET-PUFFED Miniature Marshmallows

▶ make it!

1. **PLACE** 8 cookies, flat-sides up, on microwaveable plate; top with remaining ingredients.

2. **MICROWAVE** on HIGH 30 sec. or until chocolate is almost melted. Cover with remaining cookies; press down lightly to secure. Microwave 30 sec. or until cookies are warmed and chocolate and marshmallows are melted.

3. **SERVE** warm. Or, cover and refrigerate 5 to 10 min. or until filling is set.

MAKE IT A PARTY!:
Place all ingredients in separate small bowls. If desired, add other filling choices, such as small candies and/or crushed OREO Cookies. Let the kids mix and match the filling ingredients as desired to create their own stuffed cookies!

USE YOUR OVEN:
Heat oven to 350°F. Top 8 cookies as directed; place on foil-covered baking sheet. Bake 4 min. Cover with remaining cookies; press down lightly to secure. Bake 2 to 4 min. or until cookies are warmed and chocolate and marshmallows are melted.

raspberry angel cake

PREP: 20 min. | TOTAL: 3 hours 20 min. | MAKES: 16 servings.

▶ what you need!

3 cups boiling water

2 pkg. (3 oz. each) JELL-O Raspberry Flavor Gelatin

1 pkg. (12 oz.) frozen red raspberries (Do not thaw.)

1 pkg. (7.5 oz.) round angel food cake, cut into 21 thin slices

1 cup thawed COOL WHIP Whipped Topping

▶ make it!

1.

2.

3.

ADD boiling water to gelatin mixes in medium bowl; stir 2 min. until completely dissolved. Add raspberries; stir until thawed. Pour into 9-inch round pan sprayed with cooking spray.

ARRANGE cake slices in concentric circles over gelatin, with slices overlapping as necessary to completely cover gelatin.

REFRIGERATE 3 hours or until gelatin is firm. Unmold onto plate; top with COOL WHIP. Garnish with fresh raspberries and mint, if desired.

HOW TO UNMOLD DESSERT:
Dip knife in warm water and run knife around edge of chilled dessert to loosen. Dip pan in warm water, just to rim, for 15 sec. Lift from water and gently pull gelatin from edge of pan with moistened fingers. Place serving plate on top of pan. Invert pan and plate and shake to loosen dessert. Gently remove pan.

turtle pumpkin pie

PREP: 15 min. | TOTAL: 1 hour 15 min. | MAKES: 10 servings.

▶ what you need!

¼ cup plus 2 Tbsp. caramel ice cream topping, divided

1 HONEY MAID Graham Pie Crust (6 oz.)

½ cup plus 2 Tbsp. chopped PLANTERS Pecans, divided

2 pkg. (3.4 oz. each) JELL-O Vanilla Flavor Instant Pudding

1 cup cold milk

1 cup canned pumpkin

1 tsp. ground cinnamon

½ tsp. ground nutmeg

1 tub (8 oz.) COOL WHIP Whipped Topping, thawed, divided

▶ make it!

1. **POUR** ¼ cup caramel topping into crust; sprinkle with ½ cup nuts.

2. **BEAT** pudding mixes, milk, pumpkin and spices with whisk until blended. Stir in 1½ cups COOL WHIP. Spoon into crust.

3. **REFRIGERATE** 1 hour. Top with remaining COOL WHIP, 2 Tbsp. caramel topping and 2 Tbsp. nuts just before serving.

CREATIVE LEFTOVERS:
Need some ideas for how to use the leftover canned pumpkin? Go to www.kraftfoods.com for recipe suggestions.